THIRTY

A collection of poetry inspired by
National Poetry Writing Month
2020

Mel Wardle Woodend

With Cover Art by Susan Wood

THIRTY

First Printing: 2020

ISBN: 978-1-9163695-3-5 (DREAM WELL WRITING LTD)

DREAM WELL WRITING

UNITED KINGDOM

www.dreamwellwriting.simplesite.com

A Dyslexia Friendly Publication

DEDICATION

This book is dedicated to everyone who has found comfort or inspiration through the reading or writing of poetry during the Covid-19 pandemic lockdown.

CONTENTS

ACKNOWLEDGEMENTS

The poems in this volume were created during National Poetry Writing Month 2020 – largely from the website prompts designed to inspire and encourage writers to create a poem a day over the course of a month (April 2020) accessed at http://www.napowrimo.net/.

I would like to give grateful thanks to Susan Wood for creating the beautiful watercolour cover artwork. This beautiful painting of a bee visiting sweet peas was visualised and created by Sue especially for the front cover of this book - in response to the poem 'A Balcony Visitor'.

INTRODUCTION

This is a short collection put together from the poetry I have written during National Poetry Writing Month 2020, whilst the nation, and most of the world were in lockdown due to the Covid-19 pandemic.

Picking Poems

Yesterday I went for a walk
And on the way I found
Some poems growing on the path
On worn and dusty ground.
In bright reds, violets, pinks, fuchsia,
Magnolia, green, grey,
All the words from the rainbow shone
In lexical display.

I bent to smell a small poem
And to my great surprise
It smelt of staying up all night
To see in the sun rise.
Then I sniffed another one which
Smelt of shoe leather like
A brand new pair of school sandals
Or bouncy pair of Nikes.

A childhood verse smelt of wet dog

Tail wags on summer days
And bounding through the garden hose
Chasing prism drops away.
Next poem smelt of Ginger Nut,
Malted Milk, McVitie's…
A rummage in the tin for some
Nice or chocolate bickies.

A shabby poem smelt of magic -
Torn and brown and faded,
It took me on a journey through
Wonderful, worn pages.
I stopped and picked the one poem
Growing gentle, strong, and calm,
It smelt of home and baking and
My Mum's warm outstretched arms.

#NAPOWRIMO DAY 1 prompt – Write a poem using metaphor. I chose instead to create a rhyming poem structured in quatrains.

Four Walls

Four walls of home hug us tight
And our brief loss of freedom
Means more lives will be saved as
Our nation locks down.

#NAPOWRIMO DAY 2 prompt – Write a poem about a place. I wrote about home in the form of a Japanese dodoitsu.

Lockdown

I gaze into my morning mug,
Lost, in the leaves,
Hoping for a caffeine hug to prise my eyes
At least.

The magic of hot chocolate, later in the day
With cream and a crumbly flake
Sends my eyes aloft dreaming of a winter date.
A whispered kiss and a soft gloved hand to
wipe away
My hot chocolate moustache.

I could comb the world - sift through sand
Contemplate with kangaroo and didgeridoo in a
far-off land
But I'd always want to come home to you
My rock, my cosy blanket, to be locked in
lockdown with.

#NAPOWRIMO DAY 3 prompt – Write a poem

using rhyme and words generated from a word bank. I used things around me to generate a word bank but chose to write in free verse.

Closer

If I chance upon you in a dream,
I delight upon your presence
And gently take your arm to walk with me...

Respecting the fragility of you being here
And understanding, accepting
That you being here is momentary.

As temporary
And uplifting
As life…

I see your weather worn face
Brown and tanned from the summer sun
Your eyes that crinkle at corners.

I hear your deep voice
Surrounding me with a softness
As warm as a childhood bowl of bananas and custard.

I touch your rough hand - strong from all the years spent outdoors working in your garden,
Clever and tender from hours of pure concentration as you mended and connected electrical circuits in your work,
As delicately as your held my hand when I was small.

We walk together and we talk.
You are wearing your smart grey jumper with the big folded over collar.
It may or may not have a cigarette burn somewhere on the front but that does not matter and we laugh and talk and you smile.

Your hair is combed neatly in my dream.
I am not sure where we are walking – we may be in a warehouse, or at the seaside. Those details are not important because all the details of you are clear.

You smell of tobacco smoke and of the

summer.
I don't know how the dream begins or how it ends.
Other people are in it but they fade out to insignificance

And when I wake
There is a calm stillness.
I am refreshed.

The part of me that I miss and is missing has been back.
We have spent bonus time together in my dream.
I am closer to you and I am grateful.

#NAPOWRIMO DAY 4 prompt – Write a poem based on dreams.

Distant Shores

A Set of Three Haiku

Swaying gently pine
Trees whisper through summer breeze
Calling my return

To protected park:
White sand beaches and clear seas
Safe from human spoil.

Mondrago will wait.
Patient pine cones float in seas
Conjured in my mind.

#NAPOWRIMO DAY 5 prompt – Fill a poem with twenty poetry devices. I chose instead to create a sequence of three Japanese haiku poems.

Total Eclipse

Bonnie Tyler said
It was a 'Total Eclipse
Of the Heart'. Obscured
Yet vivid as broken hearts
Beat with more strength than they know.

#NAPOWRIMO DAY 6 prompt – Create an ekphrastic poem. I chose to write a tanka instead.

Stay at Home –

Senryu

A terrified world

With orders to 'Stay at Home'

So we may survive.

#NAPOWRIMO DAY 7 prompt – Write a poem based on a news article. I structured a relevant senryu poem.

Spring

Winter bareness has

Finally dispersed giving

Way to spring blossom

The way that mesmerises

Me year after year.

Warm days are here; now we can

Bare arms and feel warmth

On skin as we work to make

Gardens of serenity.

#NAPOWRIMO DAY 8 prompt - Take a line of a well-known poem and use it as inspiration to create a new poem. I ignored this prompt and decided to write a choka poem.

Moon

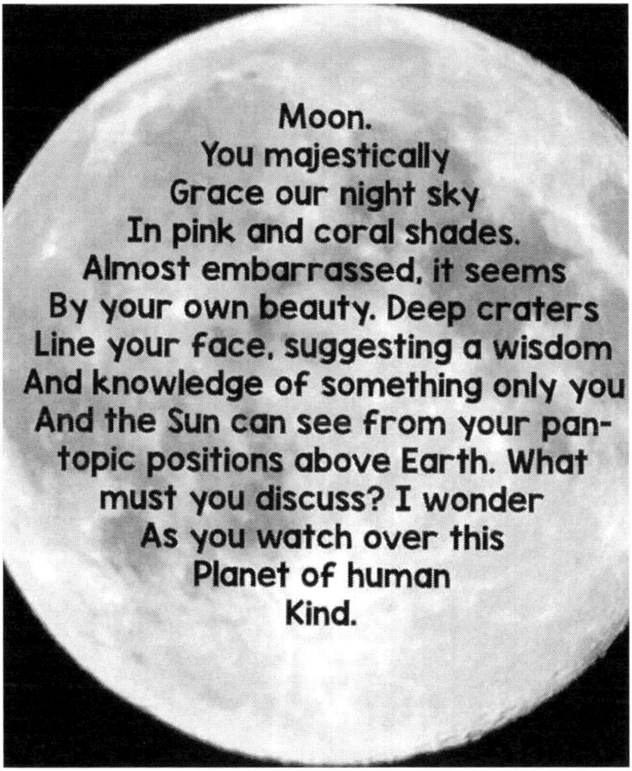

#NAPOWRIMO DAY 9 prompt – Create a shape poem. As the April blood moon was prevalent in the sky, I took inspiration from this.

Fish and Chips Hay(na)ku

Chips

With fish:

Fish, chips, peas...

Traditional

Gourmet meal

At the seaside

Or

Convenient when

In a rush.

#NAPOWRIMO DAY 10 prompt – Create a hay(na)ku poem. I chose to create a sequence of three.

The Dandelion

Yellow and magnificent,
The dandelion towers over tiny daisies on the lawn,
Who can only gaze upwards in awe
As they sit
In the shadow
Of its splendour.

The dandelion knows no bounds -
Releasing seed heads to pollinate through the breeze:
To settle in a crack between paving stone slabs
Or nestle in a grassy field.

Gardeners 'tsk' and 'tut'
At the dandelion's presence in a plant pot or on a perfectly striped lawn.
Yet, the mighty dandelion is revered!
A treat most tasty, desired by guinea pigs

across the land
Who wheek and squeak with joy at the
prospect of a freshly chopped stem,
Served with a sprinkling of yellow petals and a
sprig of green leaves
To be savoured and chomped
In sweet delight.

#NAPOWRIMO DAY 11 prompt – Write a poem using the language of flowers.

Bridge to Nowhere

We walked to the bridge to nowhere,
Over fields chapped and cracked from floods
Where patchy grass grew sparse and bare.
We walked to the bridge to nowhere,
A gentle respite in fresh air
Admiring blossoms and spring buds.
We walked to the bridge to nowhere,
Over fields chapped and cracked from floods.

#NAPOWRIMO DAY 12 prompt – Write a triolet.

Stolen

Sometimes it's unfathomable to understand how something so tiny transformed our lives,

Taking our hearts, just for you, knowing you had somehow always been destined to own us;

Oblivious to the insecurity we experienced of our own ability. Terror merged with love, fear found in responsibility.

Looking deeply into two full moons of yellow, it was as though the Moon Goddess silently urged us along a path to our peace through all the love found in your eyes.

Even now, so many moons later, your presence brings peace - the solid weight of a purring cat on top of me as I sleep is perhaps the most gentle expression of love.

Nearly fourteen years later I am grateful every day for your existence - you stole our hearts the moment we first saw your saucer eyed stare, stumpy tail, and spiky fur - and our hearts will forever belong to you.

#NAPOWRIMO DAY 13 prompt – Write a poem on the theme of stealing unapologetically. I structured mine as an acrostic.

Poets and Politicians

A Set of Three Tanka Structured Stanzas

William Wordsworth,
William Blake and Wilfred
Owen inspire through
Themes of nature juxtaposed
With war, human fail, frailty.

I wonder what they
Would make of our present world?
The arrogancy
Of leaders who believe we
Have power over nature!

Politicians who
Orate lies in metaphor.
Abuse poetic
Devices - destabilise
A country knocked off its feet.

#NAPOWRIMO DAY 14 prompt - Write a poem that deals with the poems, poets and other people who have inspired you to write poetry. I created a set of three stanzas each structured as a tanka about poets - veering off to look at relevant current political issues.

Music

Mystical bars of orchestrated beauty beat through my ears,

Under my skin where goose bumps rise

Synapses transport tingling nerves and my senses swell with emotion

I smile or cry involuntarily and am transported,

Closing my eyes and reaching in to the clarity of memories.

#NAPOWRIMO DAY 15 prompt - Write a poem inspired by your favourite kind of music. I chose to write an acrostic to spell out music, and focused on the way music affects the senses, not on a favourite musician or piece.

Day of Rest

What will I do with my day of rest?
Will I harness it, appreciate, and refresh
My body with healthy food to eat?
And catch up on much needed sleep?
Will I paint a picture, read a book?
Watch TV, or bake or cook?
Will I catch up on overdue phone calls to
neglected friends?
Find odd jobs to do and things to mend?
Will I take a walk and avoid the rain?
Listen to music to relax my brain?
Whatever I choose the choice is mine...
And to have such choice is delightfully divine.

#NAPOWRIMO DAY 16 prompt – Write a poem of over-the-top compliments. I ignored the prompt but wrote a cheerful, uplifting poem in rhyming couplets.

Robin Hood

When I was seven
You were a TV repair man.
We had two VCRs
When many people had none.

We weren't rich in money but in other ways -
I was lucky and proud to have a Dad who could repair
Anything electrical - who fixed up
Old VCRs for friends to share

Our pleasure - our electronic treasures with them.
When I was seven I was ill in hospital on a children's ward.
You brought in a video player
And a pirate copy of Robin Hood you'd recorded.

I don't remember watching the film in hospital,

Unwell I slept, lulled by the opening music right through
To the final credits but I do remember how it felt when
You came in and set it all up and how the other poorly children were excited and had their day brightened because of your kindness -
because of you.

#NAPOWRIMO DAY 17 prompt – Write a poem that features forgotten technology - maybe it is a VCR, a rotary phone, a cassette player, or even a radio. I wrote about my Dad and our experiences with VCRs in the 1980s.

Tea

The only cure for
A slow morning sleepy start
Or hangover when
Hot caffeinated liquid
Drips down dry throat - wakes
My senses, as reviving
As morning IV fluid.

#NAPOWRIMO DAY 18 prompt – Write about simple Saturday morning pleasures. I created mine in the form of a choka.

The Shell

Cream coloured cockle

Shell rounded, ridged and wedged in

Smoothed grainy sand, damp

Under bare feet as I find

Nature's treasures on the beach.

#NAPOWRIMO DAY 19 prompt – Write a poem inspired by a 'walking archive' - where you collect or have collected something on a walk. I have a cockle shell in my kitchen, collected from a beach walk last year, so used this for my inspiration.

Birthday Cake

Made with love, the cake

Rose proudly on doilied plate,

Candles sparkling.

#NAPOWRIMO DAY 20 prompt – Write a poem about a homemade gift. I structured mine as a senryu, based on the birthday cake my Mum made for my fortieth birthday.

The Sea

I Thálassa

The sea once told me

It could cast away my fears

With a gentle kiss

From salt breeze lips and arms that

Tightly wrap around my soul.

I thálassa mou eipe kápote

Tha boroúse na apomakrýnei tous fóvous mou

Me éna apaló fili

Apó ta cheili kai ta chéria aeráki alatioú

Sfichtá tylixte tin psychi mou.

#NAPOWRIMO DAY 21 prompt - Find a poem in a language you don't know and perform a 'homophonic translation' to try to translate the poem simply based on how it sounds. I ignored this prompt but wrote a tanka in English then translated it into Greek.

Squabs

Yellow and flailing
Beaks too long for tiny frames
That shiver under
Mother pigeon's fluffed feathers
'Til they grow into themselves.

#NAPOWRIMO DAY 22 prompt - Find an idiomatic phrase from a different language or culture. I ignored this prompt and wrote a tanka about our new-born pigeon squabs.

P Is For

P was for Peter Puppy of Letterland fame,
P was for three points in a Junior Scrabble
game.
P was for 1980s toy pogo sticks, Pound
Puppies, Polly Pocket and Play-Doh.
Pushing faster on a roundabout - around and
around we go!
Pooh Bear and Piglet, Play School on BBC TV:
With Poppy, Jemima, Little Ted, Big Ted, and
Humpty.
P was for parks, playing and picnics, picking
garden runner beans,
Picking strawberries at the fruit farm - stained
mouths like vampire scenes.
P was for penny sweets from the corner shop
And indoor painting at the breakfast bar until
the rain stopped.
P was for the pain of a head cracked open
from pedalling backwards on my trike,
Pitchcroft, Peter Pan play at the theatre,
watching with parents - Patricia and Mike.

Now P is for poetry and poeting,
Performances and publishing.
P is for my Mum, Patricia,
Now a pensioner.
P is for pictures on the wall of family memories past
With Sam the family dog, and Dad, and my puppy Patch.
P is for postcards kept from yesteryear,
Partying when younger - drinking too much beer.
P is for Prosecco when I'm feeling posh,
And pasta for our favourite dining out treat nosh.
Pendolino trains to London picking seats facing the right way -
Pushed together like sardines standing in the gangway on a busy Saturday.
P is for pink sweet peas, petunias,
Phlox, pansies and photinias;
Planted purposefully, and patiently grown.

#NAPOWRIMO DAY 23 prompt - Write a poem about a particular letter of the alphabet.

Bananas

Banana split,
Bananarama,
Banana milkshake,
Bananas in Pyjamas.
Banana Man,
Banana mashed,
Banana skin
In the trash.

Bananas green,
Bananas brown,
Bananas lost,
Bananas found.
Banana cake,
Banana liqueur,
Banana peel
On the floor....

Oops.

#NAPOWRIMO DAY 24 prompt – Write a poem about fruit.

Arachne

Eight
Legs run
This way and
That. You can't catch
Me! Giant human looming I
Spy you with my eight eyes
And watch which way you lunge then
I outrun you on my eight arachnid legs.

#NAPOWRIMO DAY 25 prompt – Use a long poem by someone else as a guidepost for your poem. I ignored the prompt and decided to create a poem that would work on a visual level about a spider - with one word on the first line, two on the second line, three on the third… Building up to eight altogether to represent eight spider legs.

Sky Breathes

Pastel blue crayonned
And coloured in
With white cloud pockets of air,
Cold and bumpy -
Pulling and pushing,
Buffeting and blowing.
Sky reflects its symmetry of blue
Downwards to the rumbling sea....

Its scratchy surface coloured with scribbles
Crazily coloured in all different directions.
Darker shades,
Lighter. White clouds form white horses
And underneath
The surface,
Warm and cool pockets of water gather and
pull.
Currents push and swirl.
The sea tumbles on.

And if I am fortunate enough to go again one
day
To the sea,
I will lie above its cool blue depths,
Weightless on the surface
And allow its waves to wash over me.
I will float and drift on currents
Holding me
As I gaze up
Into a safe
Sky that breathes.

#NAPOWRIMO DAY 26 prompt – Use the Alamanac poetry questionnaire. I ignored the prompt and wrote a free verse poem about the sky.

THIRTY

The Roaring Twenties

The only roar to be heard are the sounds of ambulance sirens on silent streets.
A nation locked down - the rich fed themselves - panic buying in greed - much more than they would need - leaving the poorer with not enough to eat.

Wearing PPE has become the new norm.
The only real weapons the world has. And we see brightly coloured rainbows decorated everywhere as a symbol of hope towards the passing of the storm.

A nation locked down with many financially terrified,
And some enjoying a slower pace of life that bizarrely, being furloughed provides.

Some, who can, have volunteered to shop

safely for the vulnerable.
Many, are lucky, shielded, yet day after day
NHS workers care for those who are sick - a
groundhog day of ventilators, and deaths. Will
they ever see light at the end of the tunnel?

Meanwhile, DIY haircuts trend on Twitter.
There's been a sudden increase in sales of hair
clippers.

The nation has slipped into a previously
unimaginable new way of life,
Having to 'Stay at Home' to protect lives.

Queuing outside the Co-op, shoppers stand in
line in masks and gloves,
Waiting their turn to forage for food and
essential supplies for those they love.

Only five allowed inside at any one time.
'Popping to the shop' has become a major
weekly expedition: waiting in the rain for your

turn but no one minds

Because we all understand the need to stay
safe.
We can't hug our friends - only give them a
socially distanced wave

Through screens, as we use technology to
socialise;
To see each other's faces, talk and catch up
with each other's lives.

This is the new normal for the Covid-19
pandemic of the roaring twenties...
Where the only roar to be heard are the
sounds of ambulance sirens on silent streets.

#NAPOWRIMO DAY 27 prompt – I ignored the prompt to write a poetic review, and instead, chose to write about the Covid-19 pandemic.

Finding My Whistle

When I was small
I remember, quite clearly, sitting on my bedroom floor.
The carpet purple and bright - somewhere in between the shade of a Cadbury Dairy Milk wrapper, and Turkish Delight.

White fitted wardrobes lined one wall, and opposite stood my bed
Made neatly by my Mum – on it propped against the wall sat a row of colourful teds.

I sat for hours playing games with my toys - Sylvanian Families in my dolls house, building things with Lego, or pushing Matchbox cars along - making lots of noise.

And I remember one day - I could have been four but I might have been six,

Sitting on the purple carpet, I blew through my
mouth and a wonderful whistling sound came
out of my pursed lips.

It surprised and delighted me in exciting equal
measures -
A new skill learnt - to hone and to treasure.

I still love to whistle - sometimes tunefully, or
sometimes loud and shrill,
And I will never forget my brilliant purple
carpeted childhood bedroom where I first learnt
my whistling skill.

#NAPOWRIMO DAY 28 prompt - Describe a bedroom from your past in a series of descriptive paragraphs or a poem. This prompt was suggested in relation to the description of Emily Dickinson's bedroom, written by her niece. I wrote a poem about a strong memory from my childhood bedroom in Worcester.

Animal Therapy

I could write about how handsome you look;
describe your soft, curly fur, talk about your tiny toes,
And how cute you look when you sit on your hind haunches to wash your nose.

I could describe with adjectives aplenty - your beady black and beautiful eyes, or use vivid verbs to show what you do
And build up a poetically precise picture of you.

But your real beauty isn't about how soft your fur is to the touch, or how heart meltingly cute you look: what I want to share
Is all about you being there....

Because you are my hero pig - my knight in Timothy Hay.

Your presence here with me means I have a friend to talk to every day.

You chatter back in guinea pig sounds and nuzzle into my neck

And I know I have a job to do to look after you, to respect

Your needs - a responsibility

Because you rely on me....

For food, water, shelter, snuggles

And sometimes those not so nice things like brushing tangles from your hair or bottom baths and you fidget, squeak, and struggle...

But, as you settle back calmly into my arms,

I know all will be forgiven with a cuddle and a big bit of pepper working its magic charm!

And when you zoom and popcorn happily around the room,

It's animal therapy for both me and you.

#NAPOWRIMO DAY 29 prompt - Write a paean poem (a song of praise or triumph / a creative work expressing enthusiastic praise) about a pet. I wrote about my guinea pig, Scruffy.

THIRTY

A Balcony Visitor

One of the first signs
Spring is here and summer's
Truly on its way:
A familiar buzz -
Flash of black, yellow, and white.

A balcony friend
Welcomed back year after year,
Gently visiting
Sweet peas, twirled high around a garden cane
And a fragrant lavender plant pot.

Perfumed, delicate
Delights, thoughtfully provided.
The bee drinks and falls
Drunk, into a dahlia.
Sleeps awhile in perfectly folded petals.

Then, in a flash of fuzz,
The bee wakes: zooms clumsily

Away, homeward bound!
Stopping en route for a quick
Call in at the Blue Buddleia.

#NAPOWRIMO DAY 30 prompt - Write a poem about something that return - such as swallows returning year after year.

WATERCOLOUR FRONT COVER IMAGE

BY SUSAN WOOD MAY 2020

ABOUT THE AUTHOR

Mel Wardle Woodend is a keen reader, writer and bodyboarder from the West Midlands. Her family, animals, interactions with the people she encounters on her journey, and the natural world all inspire her work. Published books include two dyslexia-friendly children's poetry books; a full-length children's story; a nature poetry collection *Natural Colours* (2017); and her most recent collection *Just a Thought* (2019) exploring mental health issues. Mel's imprint Dream Well Writing Ltd publishes dyslexia friendly books as she is passionate about ensuring reading is accessible to all.

Mel has edited and published various anthologies to support charities and organisations including: *The Friendship Collection* (2018); a set of three anthologies to raise money for Parkinson's UK, and two environmental awareness poetry anthologies for There Is No Planet B Stafford; *There Is No Planet B – Act Now* (2018) and *Global Warning* (2019), and *One Hundred Memories* (2019) in aid of Alzheimer's Society.

Mel is Staffordshire Poet Laureate 2019-2021 and works full-time as a writer, editor and performance poet: organising poetry slams and events, facilitating creative poetry workshops for adults, participating in slams and open mics, and performing at festivals around the UK; including Wolverhampton LitFest 2018 Poets Against Racism; Creativity and Wellbeing Week 2019 in London; and Worcestershire LitFest 2019.

Mel holds a Master of Arts degree in Creative Writing and has ten years' experience as a teaching assistant in primary and secondary schools. She frequently delivers children's poetry workshops in schools and libraries across Staffordshire and the West Midlands.

Her next poetry collection *Forty* is due to be published imminently.

Follow Mel's work at

www.melwoodendwriting.com

facebook.com/melwardlewoodend/

instagram.com/melwardlewoodendauthorandpoet/

twitter.com/wardlewoodend

THIRTY

PORTRAIT PHOTOGRAPH BY

'A BLIND PHOTOGRAPHER' MARCH 2020

PREVIOUS PUBLICATIONS

Poetry Collections

A Poet's Poems (2015)

Journeys and Memories (2015)

Poems of Spring (2016)

Natural Colours (2017)

Just a Thought (2019)

Children's Poetry Collections

What Am I? An Alphabet of Animal Poems (2017)

I Smell Fish and Chips and Worms Too (2017)

THIRTY

Children's Fiction

Tails of a Little Brown Mouse (2018)

Charity Poetry Anthologies

There Is No Planet B – Act Now (2018)

The Friendship Collection – Children's Collection (2018)

The Friendship Collection – Poetry (2018)

The Friendship Collection – Short Stories and Young Adult Fiction (2018)

Global Warning (2019)

One Hundred Memories (2019)

FORTHCOMING PUBLICATIONS

Novella

My Diary of a Cat Owner – coming soon….

THIRTY

DREAM WELL WRITING LTD

Dream Well Writing Ltd are publishers of dyslexia friendly books.

Find out more about Dream Well at

http://dreamwellwriting.simplesite.com/

https://www.facebook.com/dreamwellwriting/

Printed in Great Britain
by Amazon

42127794R10043